THE SCALE OF CHANGE

THE SCALE OF CHANGE

Desmond Graham

FlambardPress

First published in Great Britain in 2011 by Flambard Press
Holy Jesus Hospital, City Road, Newcastle upon Tyne NE1 2AS
www.flambardpress.co.uk

Typeset by BookType
Cover Design by Gainford Design Associates
Cover image: engraving of St Paul's London, reproduced from an
illustration to *The American Cyclopaedia* (1873) © StratoSphere 2010

Printed in Great Britain by Bell & Bain, Glasgow

A CIP catalogue record for this book is available from the British Library.

ISBN: 9781906601249

Flambard Press wishes to thank Arts Council England
for its financial support.

Flambard Press is a member of Inpress.

The paper used for this book is FSC accredited.

Contents

Class

Rembrandt's Last Pupil

For Trude and Milena

Class

My Childhood

time of princes
and monarchs
when the Shah
and empress Farah
were the goodies

and a man
like king Farouk
could morph
a few years later
to 'veruka' –

something
the Aldridge girls had
or one of them
and far too upper class
for us to be afraid of

like the lucky girls
who caught
their monarch
by their golden tresses
that noble little Jordan

like a middle-order
batsman
with sharp suits
and centuries
of peace and civilization

or like Ranier
and that great race-track
down the mountains
of Monaco

*

we were so multi
racial –
Learie Constantine
could come to me half-
Irish like my grandma

the Nabob
of Pataudi
could bat out
an English summer
made of autumn evenings

we were superior
like the Saudis
with their string
of racers
tail-coats and glasses

we could wave across
in days before the cameras
to the queen's coach
passing the post
all others at the starter's

and if our role
if role at all
we ventured
could be sentry-box
straight-faced chin-strapped

lady's-maid
or horse-proud
coachman
we were always
one of them

though they
no doubt
were never
one of us

* * *

My Father

at the cricket club
always came after
Mr Lee
and all his family
and after
Neil Corker
Eric Staunton
Tony Nunn
and all the young ones
with their little caps
and stripy blazers

he had lost his pace
and lost his length
and batted
with the front foot forward
whatever the bowler
seeing the team through
bad light
and the final over

in theatricals
he always played the butler
or in later years
the chief inspector

told where to go
by colonel squire
and family doctor
though the murderer
was always
one of them

but in church
despite Miss Blow
and Mrs Judd's
high culture
he had just God
above him
and the great composers
and his childhood
standards
when he sang
professional
Morales
Clemens (non Papa)
Beethoven in C

*

a child of London
he had brought down
with him
to the country
all those of Cheyne Walk
or Rotten Row
who gave orders to his father
now known as gentlemen
or speculative builders
banker broker
businessman or thief

while farm labourers
and council workers
trundled in
with their strong arms
to last two dozen overs
and Major Virtue
still with slatted pads
from Grace or Trumper
to bat at number three
dozed at second slip
or fumbled in the gulley
my father fielded mid-off
both ends
encouraging the bowler

he had no chevroned
colours
to his pullover
cable-stitched
hand-knitted
by my mother
wore the club cap
available to every member
and never did work out
the social order

***

I never crossed the road

the children unknown
and dangerous
over there
and what went on
behind the row of houses
I never found out

but on my bicycle
sped up the hill
and past
to turn sharp right
and through
the private gateway

where I would wait
for Celia
a place at Leeds assured
a gin and tonic
like a school-cup
in my fingers

to be questioned
by her father
'forgive my ignorance
do forgive me
but Leeds
is that at Oxford
or is it Cambridge'

* * *

Just Like Us

that good man
Dr Johnson
gave his black servant
livery
so people knew
attacking him
had little chance
to pass
unnoticed
just like our Hawk

Trainers
Meteors
and Vampires
protecting Pasha
Arab prince
and worthy rulers
from the crowds
of vulgar noisy people
who could pull them down
for two pins
just like us

* * *

Law and Order

Günter Podola
hung by the neck
until he's dead
in Wandsworth

and the gruesome crowds
outside
in silence
wishing they could see

black cap
and sentence
prison-clock and tolling bell
the signs of order

all my father's tales
of London streets
and famous murderers
turned sour

*

the Mau Mau monsters
made from nightmares
our poor soldiers
saving lonely farmers

the torturers
were always theirs
our men sent in
to sort it out

cleanly
bring them to their senses
teach them
law and order

and the hood
and drop
I measured
hoping

that the knot
was placed
with merciful
precision

our Pierrepoint
world champion
in harmless
execution –

all that took years
to tumble out
like secrets
from a drawer

as if my father's
bedside cabinet
proved him
a follower of Crippen

or the shed floor
where I played
pilot chemist
Darwinian explorer

dug-up showed
a history
like that one house
in Gloucester

and the truncheon
hung behind the door
at grandma's
from her husband –

special constable
before the first
world war –
had had a use

* * *

Reich

my betters
at the Oxbridge
Colleges
went on
to rule the empire

while I arrived
for tea and cake
with servants
for the first time
black
and heard them bullied
so much more
than those at home
who served
just like my mother
in restaurants
and shops

the foul mouths
of those English
aunts
in Africa
and even children
giving orders
like a plague
right in the face
as if nothing
notable
had happened

no problem here
the old conundrum
solved
what would have happened
to the English
under Hitler

* * *

Post-Colonial

what happened
to 'London'
waiter at the university
and part-time servant
cleaner really
mine

or the Nanny
live-in
in an outhouse
shed
beside the College flats
no bigger
than the hut
I played in
fighting Hitler

six pounds a month
plus 'boys' meat'
and so much mealy-meal
– I was on about a hundred –
with her own small child
carried on her shoulders
while watching mine

we gave them
whatever happened to
Mugabe

*

what happened
to 'Moses'
in Freetown
coming up each day
from nine till six
and disappointed
not to call me
master
and wait
in full uniform
upon our table

and the peanut girl
cross-eyed
and barely twelve
I gave sixpence
each time
I parked the car

we left them
Rio Tinto
and our love of diamonds

* * *

Sir

though at home
it was much better
still
I was 'sir'
into the nineties
dinner
on the High
and others
taking orders

how naïve
to think
of Thatcher smashing
only miners
she opened up
the back gate
added
shady dealers
sharp-voiced brokers
to the same old lot
and they got on
nicely

left the rest of us
to contemplate
our navels

* * *

Homecoming

oh green fields
and cottages
of England
lost lanes
of queen
anne's lace

where hollyhock
and delphinium
and hem-stitched borders
line the crazy paving
on the card
sent out from Barrow

and welcomed
by 'The Manchesters'
in trench mud
1916
pictured
arm in splint
and lightly bandaged
by the cottage gate

smiling

'No Place
Like Home'

* * *

The main road

where the rag-a-bone
with nag and laden cart
rang out his bell
my mother
gave out tea
to Yankees
halted
on the Portsmouth Rd
in convoys
and they threw me
little tins of malt sweets
on their way

* * *

Salvage

I stood beside
'the salvage'
five sacks
nailed up
like five graces
to re-distribute
the country's
wealth

pigswill
for bankers
pulp
for the press
old iron
for armaments
old clothes
to cover up
and for the rest
bones
to make our social
glue

***

The North

We never got past
Watford
and when we did
we were afraid
a little
and relieved
to find it
almost normal

the north
to us in talk
was Waltham Abbey
where great-grandfather
carved new pews
and made this mirror
from the old wood
he chose
as payment

our relatives
on farms
their own
around Northampton
were a strange breed
not knowing air-raids
protestant
and with their problems

cousin Phyllis
in The Grail
which sounded like
some prison
Aunty Lou at cards
in Monte Carlo   .

and the breathing
from the pantry
dead hare they said
or death from poison
taken in the bathroom
right next door

the back staircase
all night creaking
darkness
inside the house
as well as out
proved this was country

and as far north
as we would venture
the car's exhaust
flung up behind us
like people waving
to a departing liner

heading to a place
of refuge
in our case
two hours later
home

***

Graduation

My parents
coming up
for graduation
mine
thought Leeds
a grimy place
the people decent
considering
and really friendly

it made them feel
even stranger
than at home
where they were hardly
normal
but had their place
and held
their memories
of London

like a brass band
having passed
whose noise
could never leave
the peopled streets
it moved through

whose marching feet
were never
out of step
with yours
though everywhere
was silent

***

Class

in fact
is like an old-fashioned
phone bell
ringing through
an empty house
just testing
what sort of person
answers
and the English
mostly
have that ringing
in their ears
no matter how
they do not listen

class
is like a draft
of air
which cannot fail
to lift you
ever so gently
sometimes
and with full force
hold others down

*

class is a game
with letters
slid along
to re-arrange
and make a phrase
to teach you
just where you are

and you struggle
nightly
fitting in the letters
wondering
if the set you're given
cannot
make one word

*

and class of course
is another word
for the school
armoury
the farmer's
gun-rack
the poor policeman's
dog

* * *

Who owns

Purcell
who owns Byrd
who owns
the Kings College Chapel
roof
the hammer beams
of Westminster Hall
the impossible old oak
of Winchester –
the nation

who owns the nation

* * *

Cobham

How could
for years
I feel such shame
in Cobham
as a birthplace
Surrey
always finding
people at the first
took to me
or not
from false assumptions

only well past sixty
where once I rode to school
on my brand new bike
– the price
of scholarship –
changed for me
from golf-course
refuge for the Beatles
and impossibly
enclosed space
to where Whinstanley
and his fellow
thinkers
'True Levellers'
as they called themselves
declared
equality
for all

*

which plaque
marks that spot
'Here lived
Ringo Starr'
'St George's
Private'
or 'Here
before so many others
and almost everyone
was voiced
in England
the right
to be human'

I lived there
twenty years
had all my schooling
within five miles
and no one
thought it worth
a mention

* * *

Newcastle

John Lilburne
'Leveller so-called'
as he would have it
preferring
'Agitator'
chosen spokesman

educated Newcastle
'Royal Free Grammar School'
dragged by his hands
tied to the back of a cart
to Westminster
put in the pillory
and gagged there
continued
lifelong
with his demand
for 'freeborn rights'

* * *

A good number

The Royal
Grammar School
Newcastle
prides itself
in its own words
on young people
from all backgrounds
benefiting
from opportunities
provided by
its education

one hundred
are assisted
at the latest count
in some way
'a good number'
as they say

the rest
can buy
the opportunities
for twenty pounds
a day

* * *

Enclosure

ensconced
for once
or only for a day
or two
in Worcester
after Corpus Christi
just the year before
and Magdalen
from the inside

knowing such splendour
as an honoured
visitor
I asked
the cleaner
what it felt like
to live
in such a beautiful
place

it's where I come from
she replied
but most of it
is closed

* * *

The gleaner

John Clare
forerunner
stayed rustic

without his label
peasant poet
not of much use

though where his birds
found refuge
in the hedgerows

across Northamptonshire
giant combines
hoover

even the smallest
gleaner's
grain

* * *

The English Poets

Cockney Keats
famed for dying
and atrocious taste
according to the papers

just not up to
Shelley
who put him
in his place

or Byron
sending notice
that Wordsworth
was a disgrace

at least he
pined away
in Cambridge –
among 'chattering

popinjays'
he wrote –
but Keats
who studied medicine

by our lights
hardly working class
read Homer
in translation

Virgil
for himself
literate
like Shakespeare's

mother – a skill
best left to women
as the playwright's
father judged

his the nobler art
of selling
gloves
to those above him

    * * *

Work

My aunt
made hats
of such perfection
Cecil B. de Mille
or someone like him
invited her
from London

a move to Hollywood
her mother
gainsayed
she later worked
instead
for Bateys
purveyors
of high class
ginger beer
and lemonade

my other aunt
would have been called
accountant
had she been a male
she balanced books
for all The Partnership
like Peter
with his scales

such was London
and for my mother
just across the road
at Fortnums
there were years
of training
in how best
to serve the rich
without offending

and their young brother
first day as clerk
came home
and outraged mother –
'your hands
are dirty
no son of mine
does work like that'
he didn't go back
next day

* * *

Pool

we had a pool
behind the school pavilion
where those with colours
could plunge in
through hottest weather
our privilege
to freely wander
side to side there
like a private
mansion
with its element
of cold

we could prove
ourselves
above it all
to nothing
but the sounds
of our own movements
until a sense of
boredom
deepened
taking over

and we climbed out
to the edge
and stood there
like a wet dog
from a river
wanting company
and not a soul about

* * *

National Service

my elders
like my brother
discovered
how our fathers
trained to fight

close-cropped
rough-faced
from winter weather
marching
under orders

I saw them on parade
in Essex
passing out
to a kind of
dance-instruction

vowels
re-shaped
no words no syntax
just a kind of
punctuated shout

* * *

The Lit and Phil

how many Jacobins
today
walk down Westgate Road

they sold the socialist
worker
down the river

and elderly professors
still stem the tide
of dry rot

falling plaster
tilted shelving
where their predecessors

also bourgeois mostly
voted for the revolution
and against their king –

Geordies
of the seventeen-
sixties

no less than
ones today
who give their lives

to save their fathers'
fathers' empire
how many miles away

*

Yeats demanded
'Who stalked
the Post Office'

and answered
promptly
with 'Cuchulain'

well it's easy here
where Stephenson
lit up his magic lantern

you don't need
to ghost-hunt
every day

just go to Easington
and ask for everyone
who had to go away

***

Thomas Bewick

just down the Tyne
Ovingham
his churchyard
Cherryburn
his place
our Rembrandt
of crossing rivers
on stilts
pole-vaulting
to a near miss
boys' tricks
monkeys
in mirrors
everyone
having a piss

defender
of the old nag
half-strangled cat
tormented dog
and frozen shepherd
friend to the vagrant
soldier
one-legged
back from the wars

he knew
a horse could
as readily
tip its rider
into a stream
as wait for
a drunken master
but had it dig
its heels in
right under the gallows
refusing to pull away
the cart

* * *

The Duke

where the North Sea
splashes the cobles
hauled up for winter
and the eider duck
like slow sulphur
skims still water

a perfect prospect
of sea behind her
she sits against
the wall
in panic

the castle round here
still has a cast from Kafka
her husband
gardener
dead
their cottage needed
she was moved on
more easily than furniture

to where no sound of sea
could fill the space
left by
the town's blackthorn
the castle gardens
and the season's
news

* * *

The Embankment

Turner
in his little boat
with rum
and oarsman
and his back to London
passed his later years
on Chelsea Reach

they've built
the spy house there
with bare-faced splendour
point-blank cheek
where Carlyle struggled
with the revolution
– French –

and Texas
millionaires
can once again look out
contented
their green back porch
protected
piece of garden

Thomas More's
who found Utopia
here
before
a little further on
the headsman

*

the traffic roars
its fond farewells
to London
past school playground
wired higher
than a prison

along the river bank
where Sickert's
ruined Irish girl
crouched
like hundreds more
attempting to decide

and now on low tide
mud
my ancestors
could freely search
for anything
abandoned

the gulls print out
their patterns
in striped footprints
familiar
from the uniforms
convicts wore

* * *

In the dark

where the night sky
was not sky
and cloud not cloud
but smoke
from deep drawn
cigarettes
filling the stadium's
first few rows
and we heard the whine
at first
like a warning
then like some thin
Tube train
blasting into the station
as the crowd
picked up
its roar
and single words
stood out
as names

and faces
and the photo
flashed
its finish
and old rags
were thrown
to the first
dog
punters
compared
their fortunes
one hand clutching
Bovril
the other
bookies' art-work
boldly coloured
with exotic name
and number
worthless
now
except for children
like me
with their father
learning the pleasure
of a crowd
the fug of night-time
and the bright relief
so briefly taken
of a chance
of luck

* * *

The Races

Sandown
Kempton
Goodwood
and Prince Monolulu
like a print
from Rousseau
ostrich feather head-dress
magic waistcoat
oriental breeches
tipping winners
'I gotta horse
I gotta horse'

Stamford Bridge
where they lifted me
over their heads
like others
too small to see
passed down
let over the barrier
to sit snug
among rows of bath-chairs
under the oilskin
where a veteran's legs
should have been

* * *

Blues

I was blue for Oxford
my brother blue
for Cambridge
as if they heard
our shouts
even from not far
from Putney Bridge

Peabody Buildings
where the chute
stank
blew back
the breath
of everything no longer
any use

the stone stairs
were there to climb
ten flights
no matter how
the legs
protested
or how old

   *

my rose was red
my brother's white
Plantagenet
and Yorkshire
CCC
and my red
Lancaster
as much as Washbrook

our pedigree
a long-range bomber
a history of famous faces
bought with cigarettes
Richard Crookback
Henry Tudor
and the Edwards
all the same

*

we were cavaliers
not roundheads
Chelsea not Arsenal
Churchill versus Atlee
our constituencies
all coloured
blue

how much more colourful
a cause
to die for
even from the wrong side
of the railings
always
on the right side
of the road

***

Clapham Junction

where the north
was always there
and ready
waiting
but never to be seen

the only colour
Coleman's mustard
only distraction
house high
a painted Oxo Cube

the grey brick
needing cover
silvered like shrapnel
burnt
at edges

impossible windows
broken blackened
far worse than anything
they imagined
as the north

and all of it
invisible
from their carriage
window
en route to London

to be settled
for the day
at Mansion House
The Strand
Cornhill Holborn

every street
Threadneedle
where the rich
could pass through
more easily than a camel

* * *

Wren Churches

I loved them –
cleared of clutter
mainly solid blackened oak
keeping reflection
to itself

made to be seen
discreetly
teach you
for the first time
how perspective works

and if the organ
piped up its patterns
and the cupola at last
cupped hand to ear
to bring you Bach

you understood
how god was moved
out of the machine
turned into proportion
balance and scale

how measurement took over
angle and leverage
structure depth and weight
like the sentences
of Pope

repeat develop vary
pause extend
and counter
return and reinstate
then close

    *

and round the corner
as that poet dreaded
paper money
moved
so unsubstantial

long before the first
computer
all the world's wealth
passed through here
like flour down a funnel

packed and stored
and sent across the water
then sent back
multiplied
by millions

the Amerindians
the Gold Coast captives
some noble savages
located near Tahiti
paid the price

you almost hear it
if you listen closely
travelling round
St Paul's dome
as a whisper

* * *

The Surprise

Haydn
came to play
up dark stairs
near Covent Garden
a small drawing room
and crowd of local
butchers
music-teachers
friends

a surprise
in Europe
used to hordes
of lordlings
dozing through
it all
till he awoke them
with his famous
Paukenschlag

today
the Albert Hall
like a roman
colosseum
packs in
such crowds
of wandering scholars
bankers
on the cheap
assorted fans
and lovers

until they must
give way
to waving
flags
and ruddy faces
not known for silence
unless ordered
to two minutes
each November

but bursting
for the jolly Tar
arranged by
Henry Wood
and sad Elgar's
moment
of decision
Pride
Pomp
Circumstance
and War

***

Albert Dock

gaudy
as a sergeant pepper
cover
the Baghdad-Aztec
ziggurat
the Red Fort
brought back
in miniature
from Agra
some St Peter's dome

with added Tudor
and the Liver Building
Disney Classic
though not its fault

such zany love
for the muddled
moment
everything brought home
put on display
like a Bed & Breakfast
sideboard
of the family
a pair of sheep
and castanets

how perfect
an aesthetic
for the English
like a love
of liquorice
the acid colours
over-sweetened
a limited assortment
all with leather stripes
holding everything together
barely noticed
just like the lost
trade
here marked out
lest we forget
in the new museum
owning up
at the last
to slavery

* * *

Dover

the plastic flags
stuck to the wall
like wet leaves
fixed there
by wind and weather
declare
St George's Day

in little butchers'
hats and shawls
of flags for England
they cried havoc
through the streets
especially
in Dover

where Gloucester
was not blinded
by the white cliffs
and King Lear
awaited rescue
from his daughter
and the French

and the samphire
gatherer
clung on
as best he could
to what the sign calls now
the cliffs
of Shakespeare

*

and in The Eight Bells
after Sunday lunchtime
drifted on again
to evening
they greet mum
on the mobile
best mum in the world

not quite plastered yet
but soon to get there
like the men
still moaning
at the bar explaining
how they did not
really mean it

no offence intended
and the High Street
Oxfam Save the
Children Mind
The Heart Foundation
RSPCA
say this is England

and the boarded houses
where once Wordsworth
waited love-sick
Matthew Arnold
popped across from
to hear the slow
withdrawing roar

of pebbles leaving England
to be rolled back up
next tide
where the corrugated waves
give little welcome
passing over everything
that passes

and the herring gull
dives
into litter
rises
like some clumsy phoenix
adjusts it wings
and shuffles

gives out
the same sharp cry
the wedding party gives
for bride
and groom
for England
and St George

noisy
sentimental
and as every visitor
from the time of Shakespeare
onwards
noticed
prone to violence

* * *

In Elysium

all the poor of Benwell
changed
their shape
and colour
in one night

the traffic lights
let past
the glow of sari
glitter
of shalwar kameez

abandoned shops
declared
cheap messages from here
to every corner
not just vanished empire

Jimmy the butcher
prepared pigs' heads
for Philippino celebrations
dressed trotters
for Angolans

all day his mate
cut out spare ribs enough
to lay in miniature
a new pacific
railway

Halal Chippie
Mama's Kitchen
Pizza Addict Old Tehran
like French Fauves
brought in colour

and the pale-faced poor
lit up with grins
not seen since Tommies
making it
to Blighty

it was no dream
just one glimpse
on a sunny morning
where the Nurses' Home
was made a new Asylum

and language teachers
after afternoons explaining
legal terms
court orders
prohibitions

looked through
net curtained windows
way beyond exhaustion
upon a little commonwealth
of possibility

not knowing
where it lead to
or if there would be time
for it to stay

Rembrandt's Last Pupil

Arent or Aert de Gelder, born in Dordrecht 1645, trained in Rembrandt's studio for six years until Rembrandt died in 1667, is remembered as 'Rembrandt's last pupil'. The designation has a special aptness for until his death in 1727, de Gelder chose to continue painting in the style he had learnt from Rembrandt. His is an art smaller, gentler, more modest than his master's, with shorter perspectives, less grand buildings, pairs and trios of people more in close-up. There is a restraint and gentleness which is so consistent it comes across not only as a matter of temperament: it offers a way of viewing things, a politics. His people are generally engaged in something where they are out of their depth, trying to catch-on or catch-up. When angels arrive someone is generally fast asleep.

In these poems I have tried to take up this turn of mind, this way of looking. 'A Gallery of Poems' is drawn from responses to particular paintings; 'A Question of Light and Dark' sets out as a dialogue, a series of pairs and oppositions, voice and counter-voice, to develop a conversation. I have been selective, choosing my own emphases, writing from my own time and place, making secular his themes: but I have tried to remain faithful to what I imagine to be the spirit of his art, with the faithfulness not of the translator but of the admiring friend.

The Artist as Joseph

Stepfather
to whatever story
God made
giving it legitimacy
and a human face

A Gallery of Poems for
Aert de Gelder (1645–1727)

Room 1

'Belshazar's Feast'

he lurches
towards the table
like any drunk
though more restrained
than usual

a good sleep
is needed
anything
right now
before the writing
on the wall

you see
the story
always starts
a little later

and what happens
here
could always be
something else

'Esther'

what she sees
we see
in her fingers
stretched
just above
the table top

right hand
as if that moment
lifted
from some completed
piece

left hand
not quite explaining
but fingers angled
to accommodate
every doubt

'Vertumnus and Pomona'

there is one truth
and the old woman
tells it
proves
so thoughtfully
its consequence
in her lined hand
above so beautiful
an arm

the young woman
haloed with a hat
blue ribbons
frame-enough
for her thinking
face
is comfortable
in herself

the old woman
is Vertumnus
boy dressed up
by magic
putting his own case

she is Pomona
fruitfulness
balancing an apple
lightly
in her fingers
just above her lap

looking towards
another story
where this old woman
will play no part

'Lot and One of His Daughters'

he is too far gone already
can barely make it
to her proffered kiss

his left hand dabbles
like a drunk fiddler
her lip and chin

his right hand arcs
towards her
his goblet his bow

guided by her fingers
spilling his wine
into her lap

this solo
of self-love
is nearly over

every note he plays
she wrote

'A Pair of Portraits'

better to make
paired portraits

not even Delilah
not Judith
with her trademark head
not the long-haired
woman
who washed and dried
feet

paired portraits
with blank wall
between them
for each to fill
if they so wish
with their passing
look

Room 2

'The Artist's Studio'

a steady powdering
of light
and someone
almost invisible
mixing pigments

a place to sit
both of you silent

one
showing
what the other
is trying to see

with palette knife
fingers
and brush

'Homer Dictates His Verses'

the young ones
at their desks
stoop so low
to their papers
they won't have sight
left for long

what he is singing
so thin and so ancient
in his great chair
they will record
to the letter
if they have patience
strength in their fingers
and the ability
to hear

long since
he lapsed
into silence
they keep on
writing

'Portrait of the Artist as Zeuxis'

it's the same old story
the woman with an apple
who looks on kindly
and is old

he
like a would-be celebrity
ready if needed
to swallow a camera

the picture
he has made of her
is over his shoulder
and dead right

he we are told
is dying of laughter
though evidently
not yet

'Dr Faustus'

his latest trick
a blaze of light
startles himself
by its success

others
shadowed
behind him
seem less impressed

more at home
perhaps
as a blacksmith
or a quarryman

at least
he is one step
further
out of his *idée-fixe*

half-bowed
half-flinching
with a guarded
look

he must admit
there may be
more to it
than this

'Jacob's Dream'

a solitary angel
larger than life
and too far away
to see clearly
is already
on the top step

like a tired traveller
flat out
or someone drunk
on the everyday
he leans against a bank

he is at home here
eyes shut
not even curious
to know
whether the angel
is about to arrive
or depart

Room 3

'Rest on the Flight into Egypt'

drawn forwards
by desire
to make it laugh
he leans
towards the infant

the infant
reaches out
to take two armfuls
of the smile
he brings

mirroring
in miniature
what now
is only possible
in this brief pause
from flight

'The Circumcision'

a tent of light
a kind-faced
high priest
carefully
engaged

the man
with a pigeon
to distract
the infant
has moved away

it takes time
to see the woman
kneeling
hand over her face
not bearing to look

'The Song of Simeon'

like sunlight
glanced up
from water

like warmth
breathed out
from a wall

his face
like a simple mirror
angled to break light's fall

cushions
in reflection
this infant's sleep

'Portrait of Herman Boerhaave and His Family'

scholar doctor
artist's friend
a father in old age
a little shy
pensive with such blessings
and not used to
giving so much away

his daughter
holds him in her gaze
one hand on his
one hand encircled
by her mother's
like a treasured secret
though long-since
disclosed

the mother
looks towards him
arm half-raised
fingers folded open
as if to start a sentence
she has found no need
to say

'Portrait of Hendrik Noteman: Sculptor'

he wouldn't want
to be centre-
stage

a little to the side
and looking out
is simply
natural
in his case

his mallet and chisel
his hands
so familiar
with their weight
his balance of elbow
take pride of place

and all
his eyes take in
steadily
with no pretence
his hands
will deliver

Room 4

Five Scenes

1
the number
and their weaponry
their agitation
towards a simple
unarmed figure
make this
so familiar
an arrest

2
beside the man
with hands bound
two tall guards
keep up appearances
as if he might
just possibly
make a bid
to escape

3
a man in a chair
not even bothering to look
his helmeted neighbour
assessing height
and length of rope
the half-naked prisoner
is of no interest to them
they are getting it right

4
the crowd
will get the blame
even the children
dragged along for the day

a man in uniform
awaits orders

when next there is movement
if anyone cares to realize
a desperate sense
of failure to have stopped this
will have taken over

5
how heavy
a dead body
three or four helpers
taking its weight
in a length of strong cloth
easing it down

and so carefully
you would think
from their solicitude
it was not dead

The First Stone

they still claim
their rights
no doubt of it
a question of law
and order

and the question
who throws first

A Question of Light and Dark

A Way In

mostly
everybody moves sideways

carrying
their long conversations

or focuses
a pace or two ahead

what all this leads to
is in shadow

curtained
with the curtains drawn back

and there is no doubt
this is a way in

A Convention of Pastors

does St Peter
like a schoolmaster
just inside the gates
turn back
to the hairdresser
all those
with unkempt hair

does the archangel
with the sternest
of features
examine the condition
of their nails

you would think
all the choirs of angels
lined up
to test the perfection
of cut
to their trimmed
beards

they could rise
and sing
even in nightshirts
soiled
if they would give themselves
up

A Dilemma

is it best
to be invisible
to lose shape
seep into shadow

is it best
to come forward
like a messenger
and say your piece

allow
what light there is
to travel
past you

hope it will fall
on whoever
least expects it
and needs it most

The Debt Collectors

address each other
with sums
they have made

talk into sleeves
around blind corners
into their chins

one combs hairs
on the backs
of his fingers

another cleans
ears
with a pin

they grow
in hiding
like skin beetles

able to gnaw through lead
or cornered
play dead

happiest
imagining the faces
clouding

the useless fury
as their wills
are read

Facial Expression

if you gathered
the sum
of human
facial expression
into one book
they would name it
Apocrypha

for each precise
fold of brow
clouding of eyes
rounding of chin
coastline of hair
says what it says
leaving no need
for the word

an art
of the unspoken
even when it is
sometimes
so loudly
and unmistakably
said

In the Middle of Things

a hand out
or a fist
clenched

a figure in the doorway
coming in
or blocking
the outside
light

floor and ceiling
dusted
with extended shadows

or every small thing
gilded
with light

the window is open
no-one need
right now
to look out

they are all
bent over
trying to find
their place
in a book

At the School for Stone Masons

the beat of hammers
is so irregular
like a company
breaking step
to make it
over a new bridge

like a choir
of long-cased clocks
striking out
the time
of each of us

and we cannot hear
which one
even when it stops
is ours

Five Women

She is leaning
on her stick
hard
her black leather gloves
tight at the knuckles

She is tall
in the cone of her long black coat
a new kind of foliage
for winter

She
even in this
is picking her words
like sparse growth
where others
find only rock

She is ready
to lift her voice
though so often silent
to make sure even dead leaves
would understand
if they were able

and she
is bent forwards
to leave the least number of angles
for sorrow
to break through

A Trinity

neither a hole
through the heavens
nor the whole sky
its full circle
open to the eye

but past cloud
past blue
past the geography
of night

      not one thing
      beech tree
      canopy of willow
      season
      or rain

      but the earth
      its creatures
      and how to shape
      the jigsaw
      from our one piece

            invisible
            maybe
            not to be outpaced
            or read
            in headstones

            our ancestors
            all of them
            and everything they made
            or left
            in us

A Visit to the Old and Sick

she is all gold
and cymbals
except for the red
handkerchief
clutched to her chest

he is already
turned into snow
on the bed sheets

his angle of head
which was kindness
now appears
absence of strength

between her bright lights
and his darkness
are two stillnesses

hers a holding in
for the moment
of bodily strength

his
the place he has come to
rests in

arms
not quite held out
but pillowed by bedding

each hand
separately
to be held or lifted

no longer capable
of forming
an embrace

A Question of Light and Dark

it is all a question of light and dark
where the light falls
and where the dark encroaches
and how far
and towards whom

and how fathomable
does even the brightest
dazzle of light
make the surrounding dark

and how far
can the darkness
not help
but give way

sometimes
even the smallest illumination
the least colouring
however faded
is all that matters

but then sometimes
there is the brightest
of lights
and absolute dark

The Peaceful Dead

they are tucked in
in finer night-shirts
than ever
they would have chosen
for themselves

in boats
with wooden sides
too narrow
ever
to set sail

their weight
now
is dead weight
their features
closed

for one who knows
the dead
the tell-tale signs
must tell
the same tale over

for those who knew
their ways
the very likeness
of this human statue
proves they've gone away

they are vanished
taken up in ether
flown elsewhere
the one thing certain
they are not there

A Question of Scale

not of balance
but of proportion

how great
and how small

all that there is
held in the crook
of a finger

all that happens
no more than dust
by a road

how big our faces
seen in mirrors
how small
when waving back

no need to adjust
a scale
it forms around you
provided you look

and know
if you can
how long
your eyes may settle

and when
to turn back

How Much Matters

if you think you understand
what matters
go back
to that moment
before it began

you will not know
where it came from
or how
or whatever it was
exactly
which made it occur

you will know
how
previously
it was not there
how
previously
everything
seemed to be in shape

the scale of change
now
you must reckon
and how much matters
before
whatever happens
can take place

A Glimpse of Heaven

two locks only
the keys
in a coded safe

but you must first ask
a stranger
then wait

until another stranger
comes up
with impossible requests

this is not
the sphinx
you need no answer

they will share a laugh perhaps
or earnestly
set out to help

you must come back
when everyone
is out

decide then
still
to wait

it needs
only persistence
and perhaps the will of god

and what you will see
with your own eyes
you can tell others

though what you saw
would not be visible
in any other light

you can tell them
how you found it
how the whole place

opened up
door after door
and you saw

and the kind guide waited
patiently
without embarrassment
while you wept

At the Place of Healing

no one knows
what is happening

least of all those
still on their feet

if one hand gestures
to point and explain

the figure beside them
has arms folded in doubt

what could be background or short-sight
is a muddle

not one of us looks likely
to make it back to his feet

but we are still hauling
with all that is left of us

hands round the waist
of the person in front

hoping to get at least
one person up

A Poem in Acknowledgement

we must assume
our debts
as those who learn
acknowledge
their own master
as I must

not thanks
to take shelter
not thanks
so knowingly
expressed
everything of yours
made so much greater

but not silence
where silence
takes upon itself
unanswered questions
and dissolves them
in smug rest

best try to touch
in passing
as a smile
gives recognition
or downcast eyes
say just as much
and if you must
say more
apologise

that what was said
you said
though any good in it
was made
from an attempt
to listen

Notes to *Class*

Learie Constantine Sir Learie Constantine (1901–1971) born in Trinidad and Tobago, a cricketer, barrister, politician, writer and campaigner against racial discrimination, in 1954 publishing *The Colour Bar*

the Nabob of Pataudi (b. 1941) actually the 'Nawab' of Pataudi until 1971, a famous cricketer who captained the Indian test team during the sixties, educated Winchester and Balliol

Dr Johnson's . . . servant the Jamaican Francis Barber (1735–1801) to whom Johnson left his estate

Günter Podola (1929–1959) pleaded amnesia to the murder of a policeman and was the last man sentenced to death and hanged in England, 5 November 1959

Mau Mau properly the 'Kikuyu Central Association', freedom fighters in Kenya's struggle for independence, widely reported as engaging in acts of terror, particularly against farmers settled from Britain; the British atrocities were acknowledged more recently (on this period of Kenyan history see Ngugi Wa Thiong'o *Dreams in a Time of War* 2010)

Pierrepoint Albert Pierrepoint (1905–1992) often referred to, though incorrectly, as the last official British hangman

house in Gloucester Cromwell Street where the victims of Fred and Rosemary West were discovered in 1994

Whinstanley Gerrard Whinstanley (1609–1676) leader of the *True Levellers*, more commonly called the 'Diggers', cultivated common land on St George's Hill near Cobham, claiming the rights of all to property (1649). They are popularly regarded as the first practitioners of communism

John Lilburne (1614–1657) radical thinker and a leader of the movement for 'freeborn rights' named by its opponents 'The Levellers'

A good number this phrase, together with all the wording of the poem's first paragraph, is drawn from the official website of Newcastle's Royal Grammar School, 2010

The Lit and Phil The Literary and Philosophical Society founded in Newcastle in 1793, first women members 1804 (members of an earlier society voted for the American Revolutionaries)

Yeats demanded 'Who stalked the Post Office' a re-working of the question asked in Yeats's poem 'The Statues' – 'When Pearse summoned Cuchulain to his side,/What stalked through the Post Office'.

Prince Monolulu a colourful and witty racing tipster of the thirties and forties often referred to as the most famous black person in Britain at that time. In fact Peter Carl Mackay (1881–1961), he was born in the Caribbean and took on his colourful name with the claim that he was a Prince of Abyssinia: his autobiography was named after his catch-phrase 'I Gotta Horse' (1950)

as that poet dreaded Alexander Pope (1688-1744) 'Epistle to Lord Bathurst' ('Of the Use of Riches'):

> Blest paper-credit! last and best supply!
> That lends Corruption lighter wings to fly! . . .
> A single leaf shall waft an army o'er . . .
> A leaf, like Sibyl's, scatter to and fro
> Our fates and fortunes, as the winds shall blow

where once Wordsworth waited travelling back and forth to a France in turmoil after the Revolution had turned into 'The Terror' – 'Here on our native soil, we breathe once more . . .' ('Composed in the Valley near Dover on the Day of Landing')

Elysium an echo of Schiller's 'Ode to Joy', used by Beethoven in his Ninth Symphony

Acknowledgements

I would like to thank the editors of the following magazines in which poems here first appeared, often in slightly different versions: *The Antigonish Review* (Canada), *Assent, The Frogmore Papers, The Interpreter's House, London Magazine, Other Poetry, Rialto* and *Staple*.

I am deeply grateful to the Keeper of the Royal Bavarian Collection at Schloss Aschaffenburg who went far beyond professional generosity on my unannounced visit, to show me, deep in the castle vaults, the surviving paintings from de Gelder's masterpiece, his Passion series. There is no catalogue in English for de Gelder's work but there is a fully illustrated catalogue (text in German and in Dutch) to the 1999 exhibition in Cologne and Dordrecht. Individual works by de Gelder can be readily found in galleries throughout the world and most can be viewed on the internet.

My personal and professional thanks must, happily, be given once again to those who have helped my recent collections: to Carol Rumens, a wonderful reader of poems and inspiring friend; to Edward Martin, who understands English as deeply as friendship; to Neil Hairsine who sees; to Tara Bergin and Alan Turnbull who understand how things are made; to colleagues and friends in Germany and Poland, for nourishment essential to writing; and to all my friends at Newcastle University. I thank Peter and Margaret Lewis, and Will Mackie, at the remarkable and sustaining Flambard Press; Gordon and Wilma Meade for years of shared making; and, finally, Trude and Milena, to whom this book is dedicated, with love.